Handmade Clay Crafts

Decorative Techniques & Projects

Handmade Clay Crafts
Decorative Techniques & Projects

by Susan Alexander & Taffnie Bogart

Sterling Publishing Co., Inc. New York
A Sterling/Chapelle Book

Chapelle, Ltd.

Owner: Jo Packham
Editor: Ann Bear

Staff: Areta Bingham, Kass Burchett, Rebecca Christensen, Marilyn Goff, Shirley Heslop, Holly Hollingsworth, Shawn Hsu, Susan Jorgensen, Pauline Locke, Barbara Milburn, Linda Orton, Karmen Quinney, Rhonda Rainey, Leslie Ridenour, and Cindy Stoeckl

Photography & Styling: Susan Alexander and Taffnie Bogart

If you have any questions or comments please contact:

Chapelle, Ltd., Inc.
P.O. Box 9252
Ogden, UT 84409
(801) 621-2777
(801) 621-2788 Fax

10 9 8 7 6 5 4 3 2 1

First paperback edition published in 2000 by
Sterling Publishing Company, Inc.
387 Park Avenue South, New York, N.Y. 10016
Originally published under the title
Charming Handmade Clay Crafts
© 1998 by Chapelle Ltd.
Distributed in Canada by Sterling Publishing
c/o Canadian Manda Group, One Atlantic Avenue, Suite 105
Toronto, Ontario, Canada M6K 3E7
Distributed in Great Britain and Europe by Cassell PLC
Wellington House, 125 Strand, London WC2R 0BB, England
Distributed in Australia by Capricorn Link (Australia) Pty Ltd.
P.O. Box 6651, Baulkham Hills, Business Centre,
NSW 2153, Australia
Printed in China
All rights reserved

Sterling ISBN 0-8069-4988-0 Paper

About the Authors

Photo by Tara H. Bogart

Taffnie Bogart, Mary Heather and Susan Alexander, with their dog Willie.

Taffnie and I met and immediately began to "meld" our ideas in 1990. What serendipity! We are both avid collectors of frips, fraps, and whatnots. Taffnie playfully began making jewelry, then sconces, lamps, plates, and bowls. A friend noted that we two are sublimely compatible. Our style has been described as quaint, charming, romantic, in a word, enchanting. Though our palettes differ, our work when placed side by side is highly complementary.

I have been working in clay for 16 years and have had my own studio for 10. In all this time, I have not even begun to exhaust all the possibilities. There is always so much to do. I am not limited by ideas, but how much time there is to work.

The years have brought us all closer together. The clay work we do is labor intensive. Our families have necessarily been joined, creating a richness we cherish. Support from our husbands, Jamie and Bruce, has made it possible for us to experiment and grow while continuing to nurture and raise the children, Kyle, Mary Heather, and our big girl, Tara.

In these times of hurry up, mass produced, franchised hecticness, it is essential to remind ourselves of simple truths – love, duty, work, and rest. There is something comforting about starting the day with a cup of tea drunk from a handmade cup – something hands created, and unique. If you make things you love, people will respond to that. It's honest. We can't think of anything we'd rather be doing.

Susan Alexander and Taffnie Bogart

Thank Yous

Kathy Dankert hangs up the work aprons worn by her in project photos.

❧ Love, love, love to Jamie, Kyle, Mary Heather, and Bruce...we adore you.

❧ Dear daughter, Tara Heather Bogart, thanks for our smarmy, *Natural Portrait.*

❧ To Harmar Kates for knowing the difference between frips, fraps, and rubbish.

❧ Colleen Heather Rogan, we love you, Dear Svengalina.

❧ To Victoria Vonier of *Private Gardener,* for introducing us to Colleen.

❧ To our model, Kathy Dankert, who came running when it was sunny, and brought more light with her.

❧ To my mom, Mary Singleton, for introducing me to *mud* at an early age, and for never minding my inspired messes.

❧ To Peggy and Paul, for neighborliness and for the fresh, hot buns.

❧ To Mary Engelbreit for liking our story and putting it in your wonderful magazine – that's how we got to do this book.

Table of Contents

Introduction 10
Getting Started 11
Techniques, Terms & Tools 12
Glossary of Colors .16
Step by Step 18-105
   A Clay for Everyone 19
   Pins 20
   Cross Box 26

Cross Box Glazing Instructions 38
Cache – Coil Pot with Pinched Flowers 42
Cache Glazing Instructions 50
Morning Glory Bower 54
Leaf Dish 58
Pinched Flower Finial 66
Cut Petal Flower Finial 71
Lattice Basket (Bowl) 76
Stamped Buttons 84
Cut Buttons 88

Pressed Buttons 92
Bottle Chiller 96
Projects 106-119
Knobs 106
Small Leaf Pot 107
Chicken Planter 108
Wee Clay Hats 111
Tile 112

Mirrors & Frames 113
Slump or Hump Molded Plates & Bowls 114
Little Chickens 115
Shoes 116
Curtain Tiebacks 117
Nest & Eggs 118
Scrap Pot 119
Gallery of Possibilities 120-126
Metric Equivalency Chart 127
Index 128

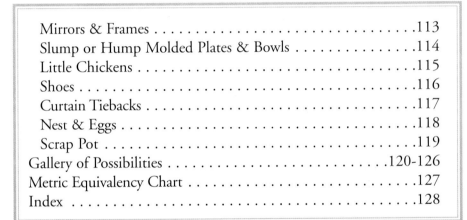

Introduction

This is a book of inspiration – a general how-to of handbuilding with clay. It is not an authoritative, technical manual, but rather a playful guide to creating decorative and functional clay art. In a lifetime you could not exhaust all the possibilities. We will show you handbuilding techniques for working with clay that may be applied to countless projects other than those we have shown you here.

To make durable, permanent, items out of clay, you need only know a small body of general information. The most rudimentary necessities include clay, water, and fire (or heat). Clay and water are shaped and when dry, fired in a kiln, glazed or embellished with color, and fired again. The rest is practice and experimenting.

People have been working in clay for thousands of years. The past and the present are bound together. Our advice to anyone who wants to work with clay is, do it. Take some clay and get busy. If there is not a public clay studio in your area, any small space, not your kitchen, will do. Sound easy? You are right! To work simply with clay is possible and can be fulfilling. It is to many people. If you have no possible access to a kiln, there are a number of air-dry and oven-bake clays available (see page 19).

Potters have been using simple tools for thousands of years. Stones used for smoothing have been passed down through generations. The sun was used to dry, and dung to fire. What could be more simple? Many cultures believe the earth is sacred and offer something in return for the privilege of using it – respect for the earth.

Yes, working with clay can become very complex if you want to airbrush, extrude, mold make, and throw. There are also a myriad of exotic glazing and firing techniques. But you will see here, clay tools are by nature very simple and much can be accomplished with basic skills.

Getting Started

Clay is a wonderful malleable medium. Within these pages, we share just a few of the infinite possibilities. There are a few basic techniques with which you can create anything.

First, a word about clay. Clay is earth. These tiny-wafer shaped particles, when surrounded by water, are flexible, and as they dry, they shrink. You can form the clay into any shape you like when it's wet. However, it should be no thicker than your thumb or about 1". Air can get trapped in the clay walls and explode during the firing process. Also, a thick wall retains water and when heated turns to steam, which also explodes during firing. This can be prevented by making things thin or hollowing them out. Bagged clay from the factory has no air bubbles. Projects in this book use clay right out of the bag. However, clay can be used over and over. Keep scraps moist in plastic and knead before reuse to eliminate air bubbles (see Knead, page 13).

When attaching clay to itself, it sticks while it's wet, but when it's dry, it will just fall off. Either score it or smooth the joints (see Scoring, page 14). For example, applying a flower to a lip of a pot…score both surfaces, apply slip, and stick together (see Slip, page 14).

There are many different kinds of clay – porcelain, stoneware, earthenware, salt clay, and raku, just to name a few. They all have different qualities and properties. The work shown in this book, except for the chicken planters and morning glory bower, is made with white earthenware (see photo, pages 108-109 and 54, respectively). The planters are terra cotta. The bower is made of oven-bake clay. Terra cotta and earthenware are low fire clays. Glaze and underglaze colors appear much darker on terra cotta; therefore, we prefer the white clay. We bisque fire to cone 04 and glaze fire to cone 06 or 05. Always make certain you know to what temperature the clay you are using should be fired. Glazes also are designed to mature at specific temperatures. Pyrometric cones are used to determine this (see Pyrometric Cones, page 14). Projects are the emphasis of this book, so kiln operating instructions have not been included. See manufacturer's instructions or a book specifically dedicated to kiln use for instructions.

If you have no possible access to a kiln, there are also plastic, air-dry and oven-bake clays that have many of the same qualities as natural clay (see photo, page 15). The oven-bake clays require no kiln and finishing takes only a few minutes…with only one baking (see page 19). Paint it and voilà.

Natural clay is workable for shaping while it's moist and flexible. Clay work before firing is called *greenware*. When dry, it is at its most fragile state. The first firing or bisque takes about ten hours, during which time the clay is heated slowly and allowed to cool slowly. The bisqueware can then be glazed. After glazing, the piece is fired again to mature the glaze. Glaze sticks to whatever it touches during firing, so most pieces are not glazed on the bottom. If the integrity of a piece requires it be glazed on the bottom, then stilts can be used (see Stilt, page 15).

Never eat, drink, or smoke in your clay working area. Wear an apron and always wash your hands after working/playing with clay. Remember, any tools from the kitchen should be retired from further food use once they have been used in clay.

Expertise takes time. Experiment! After all its only mud and time.

Techniques, Terms & Tools

Many clay tools are like cooking tools. Any tools from your kitchen such as a rolling pin, meat tenderizer, garlic press, or wooden spoons can be used. Once used to work in clay, they should be retired from future food use.

Apron
An apron is a good idea, as clay and glazes are dusty. Aprons help keep the dust contained.

Bisque Fire
The first firing (heating slowly) in the kiln to harden the clay before glazing.

Brushes
You will be rewarded with success if you have good brushes. Good tools make any project easier.

Brush Care
Good brushes are an investment. Never leave brushes soaking in water. It bends the bristles, the handle swells up, and the ferrule stretches, then when the brush dries the ferrule becomes loose and the handle slips out…oops this brush is history. To clean brushes, gently work bristles with fingers while rinsing, give them a new *hairdo* by shaping with fingertips and store bristle end up (see photo below).

Carpenter's Square
12" x 8" right angle metal measuring device. Used to measure and achieve a true right angle.

Circle Cutter
Like a cookie cutter with a plunger (see photo, page 85).

Left to right: 2" China bristle, ¼", flat, #11 round, #9 round, #8 round, #4 round, #1 round, #00 round

Clay Cutter
A length of fish line strung between two handles, buttons, beads, metal washers, or whatever is handy (see photo, page 29). Used to slice off large chunks of clay.

Coil
A long rolled out piece or "snake" of clay.

Coiling
Technique used to build up the walls of the piece you are creating. They can be smoothed so the coils disappear.

Firing
The heating process in a kiln. We bisque fire to cone 04 and glaze fire to cone 06 or 05. Always make certain you know to what temperature the clay and glaze you are using should be fired.

Fork
Used for scoring two clay surfaces to be attached to each other. (Once used for clay, retire from food use.)

Glaze
A mixture of ground minerals and oxides suspended in water. It is usually applied to a bisque surface to enhance and seal the clay. If applied to greenware, it is not water tight.

Glaze Fire
Once glazed, heating of the bisque clay work in a kiln to melt the glaze. We glaze fire to cone 06 or 05. Always make certain you know to what temperature the glaze you are using should be fired.

Glazing
Applied onto a bisque-fired piece by brushing, pouring, or dipping (see Glazing Instructions, pages 39 and 51).

Greenware
Dry clay piece which has not yet been bisque fired.

Hump-molding
Laying a clay slab over a molded plaster form or any shallow plate or bowl. Sometimes referred to as a "drape mold."

Kiln
A high temperature oven for heating clay. Projects are the emphasis of this book, so kiln operating instructions have not been included. See manufacturer's instructions or a book specifically dedicated to kiln use for instructions.

Knead
Press clay with fingers and heals of hands in a rocking, circular motion to re-use clay and eliminate air bubbles.

Leather Hard
Stage of drying where clay piece is soft enough to be carved, and stiff enough to retain its shape.

Loop/trimming Tool
A wire loop with wooden handle for scooping, hollowing, and trimming (see Tools photo, page 14). These come in all shapes and sizes.

Matt Glaze
A dull surface glaze.

Needle Tool
A long, sharp point with wooden or metal handle.

Palette
A surface to mix glaze or paint colors on. We use old white plates. (Once used for clay, retire from food use.)

Pearl   Pearl
Wherever the pearl symbol is shown, it indicates a helpful tip we refer to as a pearl (as in Pearl of Wisdom). Watch for pearls here and there.

Pencil
Pencils (with dull, medium, and sharp points) are handy, versatile tools, enabling you to achieve any thickness of line. A needle tool is just too sharp for most drawing done on clay.

Pinching
Pinching is just what it sounds

like. Take the clay in between your fingers and pinch into whatever shape you want. If what you want is thicker than your thumb, the piece is then hollowed out. Use a loop or trimming tool to hollow out. Walls should be less than 1" thick.

Pyrometric Cones
Small, triangular cones made of ceramic materials that melt at specific temperatures. They are used in determining the inner temperature of a kiln.

Refractory
Materials resistant to melting (stilts, kiln shelves, posts, and bricks).

Rolling Pin
A cylinder of wood about a foot long with handles for rolling out clay. (Once used for clay, retire from food use.)

Ruler
A basic tool used for measuring out patterns and cutting a straight edge of clay.

Scissors
Craft scissors for cutting out patterns are sometimes needed (see photo, page 28).

Scoring
The scratching of two clay surfaces with a fork or needle tool before joining.

Slab
A flat sheet of clay, used to handbuild ($\frac{1}{8}$" to $\frac{1}{2}$" thick for the purpose of this book).

Slip
Very wet, soupy clay used to join scored pieces together.

Slump-molding
Laying a clay slab inside of a molded plaster form, or any shallow plate or bowl.

Small Roller
$1\frac{1}{2}$" wide wooden roller with handle. It's a seam roller for wall-papering (see Tools photo below).

Soft Clay
Clay that is not too wet, not too

Tools

Pencils

dry – just right for pinching, modeling, rolling out slabs, coils, and impressing leaves or fancy lacework.

Spackle
Softening rough edges by wiping piece gently with a damp brush or sponge when it is dry.

Pearl *If there are rough spots or edges on your bisque piece, they can be sanded with sandpaper. However, it is much easier to remove blemishes before bisque firing, when the clay is still green.*

Sponge
Natural and synthetic sponges come in different sizes. Use the shape and size that fits your needs.

Stamps
Tools used for making textures, clay stamps can easily be made by shaping a small knob of clay with a flat surface. When the flat surface is pressed on any relief (lace, shell, button, or whatever), it takes on that texture in reverse. For example, if you wanted to make a stamp with your initials, the letters need to be backwards on the stamp. Air- and oven-baked clays make great stamps - and are quick too!

Stilt
A piece of refractory with high temperature wire nubs that hold the work off the kiln shelf. The small nubs just leave a tiny mark that can be sanded smooth.

Thin Plastic
The kind of plastic dry cleaners use. It is very flexible and drapes nicely over or under the clay without leaving wrinkle marks.

Underglaze
This is similar to matt glaze. It colors the surface, but does not seal the clay. A clear glaze may be applied over underglaze to make it shiny and water tight. Underglazes may be mixed to achieve a watercolor-like effect. It may be applied to clay in a bisque or green state.

Wooden Meat Tenderizer
A kitchen utensil used for creating texture. (Once used for clay, retire from food use.)

Wooden Paddle
A flat wide wooden paddle is used to firm together clay seams (see photo, page 34).

A few examples of oven-bake and air-dry clays available.

Glossary of Colors

Lavender Thistle

Purple Coneflower

Coral Trumpet Vine

Double Hollyhock Pink

Magenta Bittersweet

Corn Husk Buff

Amber, Jade & Cobalt

Hen-n-Chicks Green

Corn-on-the-Cob Yellow

Pumpkin Orange

Sunflower Yellow

Leafy Green

When choosing colors for glazing, we are inspired by nature.
Here are some examples of what inspire us.

Coral Zinnia

Magenta Zinnia

Black-eyed Susan Yellow

Fox Tail Green

Snapdragon Apricot

Lavender Cosmos

Golden Rod Yellow

Orange Wildflower

Apple Red

Crabapple Red

Hydrangea Cream

Soft Viola Purple

Step by Step

The projects in this section guide you step by step to making beautiful handbuilt works of art. We consider handbuilding with clay to be an art form, not just a hobby. These projects have been carefully selected to develop skills that can lead to more complex projects. After you learn the techniques, build on them with your own ideas.

A Clay for Everyone

Whether or not you have access to a kiln, there is a clay for you (see photo, page 15). The projects in this book may be used with clay either requiring a kiln, oven, or air to dry. Each project indicates the appropriate clay with the following symbols.

✳	≡	🍃
Kiln-Fire	**Oven-Bake**	**Air-Dry**

Additionally, kiln-fire clay comes in a wide variety of colors and types such as terra cotta, porcelain, stoneware, and white earthenware. The majority of the projects shown in this book are made of white earthenware (see Getting Started, page 11).

The pins below are shown as finished kiln-fired, oven-baked, and air-dried pieces (see Step by Step Instructions, page 21). The differences in construction can be applied to all our projects. When using oven-bake and air-dry clays, always follow manufacturer's instructions carefully for best results.

Kiln-Fire ✳

Once a kiln-fire clay project is constructed, it must be dried slowly to prevent cracking and bisque fired. After the bisque firing, underglaze and glaze can be applied. The piece then must be kiln-fired again (see Glazing Instructions, pages 39 and 51).

The edges of a kiln-fire clay may be refined after the clay is dry, but before it is bisque fired (see Spackle, page 15).

Oven-Bake ≡

Oven-bake clay picks up debris easily, so always work on a clean surface. If you work on paper, use paper with no print.

No scoring is necessary for joining pieces. Press firmly to join, removing visible seams. After baking, acrylic paints can be applied. Apply two coats of crystal clear acrylic coating to give it a shiny, glazed look.

Refining the edges is not needed, but may be sanded after baking.

Air-Dry 🍃

Air-dry clay picks up debris easily, so always work on a clean surface. If you work on paper, use paper with no print.

No scoring is necessary for joining pieces. Press firmly to join, removing visible seams. After drying, acrylic paints can be applied. Apply two coats of crystal clear acrylic coating to give it a shiny, glazed look.

Refine edges after the clay is dry (see Spackle, page 15).

style stateside. Our editors hav[e]

pottery to a pretty bedroom de[

floral

Brun

of the

boutis-i

antique

of vary:

to get j

already

we do.

WATERCOLOR BY MARGARET KENNEDY

Pins

Hats need adornment. Vests need souping up. Use ...cy to add texture to your pins.

Pin back (found in most craft stores)
Rolling pin (Once used for clay, retire
   from food use.)
Small bowl of water/sponge
Small roller
Small ruler

...a good way to utilize slab scraps.

Slice off about 8 oz. of clay with a clay cutter. Roll out clay with a rolling pin to ¼" thick slab, to desired size (see photos, page 29). Press lace into clay with a small roller.

Peel lace design from clay.

Cut out shape with a needle tool.

Create edge texture by pressing lace or other design on clay edge.

Press against the edge of the clay design with a small ruler, if a straight edge is desired.

Smooth edges with a damp sponge or finger.

Dry slowly to prevent cracking. Bisque fire to recommended temperature. Glaze and glaze fire (see Glazing Instructions, pages 39 and 51). Attach pin back so lock closure faces down, slightly above center, with epoxy glue.

Wee Clay Hats can be turned into pins by attaching a pin back with epoxy glue (see page 111).

Tiles can also be decorated with lace impressions (see page 112).

Cross Box

Imagine a windowsill lined up with cross boxes – each presenting a fresh geranium, African violet, or miniature roses.

Materials ✳

Clay, about 4 lbs.
Carpenter's square
Clay cutter
Fork (Once used for clay, retire from food use.)
Lace (or something for texture)
Marker, black medium point
Needle tool
Paper for pattern
Pencil, dull point
Rolling pin (Once used for clay, retire from food use.)
Ruler

Scissors
Small bowl of water
Small roller
Sponge
Stamp or button for texture
Wooden paddle

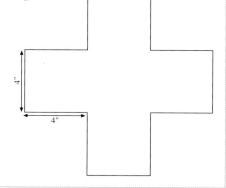

Make the above pattern with paper, a marker, and a carpenter's square. Cut out with scissors.

To cut clay with a clay cutter, grasp and pull toward you through the chunk of clay. Slice off about 4 lbs. of clay.

Roll out clay with a rolling pin to ⅓" thick slab, about 14" x 14".

Place pattern on clay. Cut around pattern with a needle tool.

Remove pattern and extra clay.

Place lace edging on clay.

Inscribe edges of clay by gently rolling with a small roller. Try not to squish out of shape.
(You may want to practice on a scrap of clay.)

Pearl *If edge of box needs to be straightened, this may be done by pressing with a ruler.*

Score base with a pencil point and ruler (to make folding easier), by drawing pencil across the bottom where edges fold up. The needle tool is too sharp and would cut the piece.

Flip over and score edges (not top) with a fork.

Fold edges up.

Paddle to firm together smoothly.

Roll a small amount of clay between palms into a ball. Score the back of the small ball and spot on box with needle tool.

Moisten ball with damp finger.

Apply slip and press onto scored area on box.

Press on with stamp or button.

If you want box to be watertight, roll out a small clay coil. Press firmly into corners.
Smooth with a finger or the eraser end of a pencil.

36

Dry slowly to avoid cracking. Bisque fire to recommended temperature. Glaze and glaze fire (see Glazing Instructions, pages 39 and 51).

Shown here are two finished boxes using these techniques.

Cross Box Glazing Instructions

Glazing can be daunting and time consuming, with experience you will find that every moment spent glazing is rewarded!

Materials
Clear glaze
Palette (white plate or plastic lid)
Soft #8 round brush (to apply glaze
    next to detailed areas)
Soft ¾" flat brush (for large areas)

Sponge
Underglaze in desired color(s) (We used
    pea green, peach, and honey – cone
    06/05.)

Glaze ingredients melt together in the kiln to form a glass-like surface. If applied too thick, glaze will drip or run, creating a nightmare on the kiln shelves, and an undesirable surface. Glaze sticks to whatever it is touching when fired. Thus, the bottom of the work should remain clean and free of glaze. If you wish to glaze the bottom, stilt the piece if possible (see Stilt, page 15).

Apply underglaze with a soft brush. Allow underglaze to dry between coats. Thickness determines intensity of underglaze and glaze color. Underglaze colors may be mixed to achieve interesting effects. To create unusual effects, you can also splatter, flick, sponge, or dribble glaze or underglaze. Clear glaze requires two flowing coats to be shiny and watertight (follow manufacturer's instructions). One thin coat will create a matt surface. Any slopped glaze wipes off with a wet sponge.

Underglaze may be mixed on palette or used right out of the jar.

Brush underglaze into the texture at top of the box with #8 round brush.

Wipe underglaze off top of lace texture with a damp sponge, leaving the color in the relief to enhance texture.

Apply underglaze in a complimentary color to interior with ¾" flat brush. Underglaze should be applied in a smooth even coat, let dry. Apply 2-3 flowing coats of clear glaze with soft ¾" brush to areas you wish to have shiny.

Pearl *A rough or stiff brush will make it difficult to achieve a smooth even coat.*

imprinted (pressed-in) lace

Glaze fire to recommended temperature (in this case cone 06/05).

Cache – Coil Pot with Pinched Flowers

From Webster's, "Cache (kash) – a store of provisions or treasures…" Use it to hold ribbons or the summer's last golden raspberries.

Materials ✳ ≡* 🍃*

Clay, about 4 lbs.
Circle (anything round to cut around)
Clay cutter
Fork (Once used for clay, retire from food use.)

Needle tool
Rolling pin (Once used for clay, retire from food use.)
Small bowl of water
Tongue depressor

Pearl *The handle on the photo opposite is made from a weeping willow whip.*

* Not for food use.

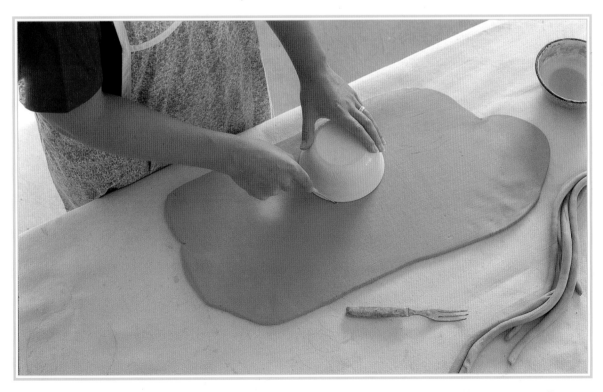

Slice off about 4 lbs. of clay with a clay cutter. Roll out clay with a rolling pin to $\frac{1}{3}$" thick slab, large enough to fit circle (see photos, page 29). Place a circle (we inverted a bowl) on slab, cut around with needle tool.

Score edge of the circle with a fork. Roll coils about ½" thick. Score bottom coil (to make certain the pot will be watertight).

Add coils by placing around on top of each other to form a straight wall about 4" to 5" tall.

Smooth coils on outside with a tongue depressor.

Repeat previous step on inside.

Decorate lip of cache with pinched flowers and leaves. To make a rose, roll a small ball of clay between palms and pinch flat.

Twist into a cone. Roll out more small balls, flatten to shape petals.

Arrange petals around cone.

Pinch bottom of flower with fingers. Cut off extra clay with needle tool. Score flower bottom and lip of pot where it is to be attached. Apply slip and squish together.

Make coil handles, leaves, buttons, and bugs – or whatever! Score, apply slip, and attach to pot. Dry slowly to avoid cracking. Bisque fire to recommended temperature. Glaze and glaze fire (see Glazing Instructions, pages 39 and 51).

The technique of coiling can be used to make an endless variety of projects, including these chicken planters (see instructions, page 110).

Here is a coil pot made without handles.

Cache Glazing Instructions

So many possibilities! To help gain confidence, practice on bisque scraps.

Materials

Clear glaze

Palette (white plate or plastic lid)

Soft ¾" flat brush (for large areas)

Soft #1 round brush (for details)

Soft #8 round brush (to apply glaze next to detailed areas)

Soft #11 round brush (for clear glaze)

Underglaze in desired color(s) (We used aqua, blue green, Dutch blue, lake blue, lavender, leaf green, light pink, medium blue, orange, purple, rose, shell pink, tawny, turquoise, white, and yellow – cone 06/05.)

Underglazes may be mixed on a palette, or used right out of the jar.

Apply underglaze on body with ¾" flat brush. Let dry between coats.

Apply underglaze with a #8 round brush when near leaves and flowers.

Apply underglaze in desired colors to flowers and leaves with #1 round brush.

Apply a smooth, even coat of clear glaze to the rest of cache with #11 round brush for a nice shiny effect. It is not necessary to glaze the outside bottom of the pot, as glaze sticks to whatever it touches when fired. Glaze fire to recommended temperature (in this case cone 06/05).

The flower construction technique in this project may be used to make knobs for drawer pulls or these jewelry organizers (see page 106).

Morning Glory Bower

Morning, noon, and night our bower of morning glories is ever blooming, untouched by frost or blight.

Materials ☀* ≡ ❦*

Clay, about 2 lbs.
Needle tool
Paints, acrylic in desired color(s). (We used alizerine crimson, burnt sienna, cadmium yellow, chromium oxide green, cobalt blue, portrait pink, thalo green, titanium white, and yellowish green.)
Pencil, medium point
Plate or circle shape
Rolling pin (Once used for clay, retire from food use.)
Small bowl of water

* The technique for kiln-fire and air-dry clays is the same, except you must score kiln-fire clay and apply slip to attach flowers and leaves to bower. Then follow firing and glazing instructions (see pages 19, 39, and 51).

Pearl *When working with oven-bake clay, always work on a clean surface, as oven-bake clay easily picks up debris (see page 19).*

Oven-bake clay comes in rectangular chunks. Work three chunks (about 2 lbs.) into a ball. Flatten with palms. Roll out clay with a rolling pin to ¼" thick slab, about 6" x 11".

Cut an 8" arch about 3" wide with a needle tool, using a plate or other handy circle shape.

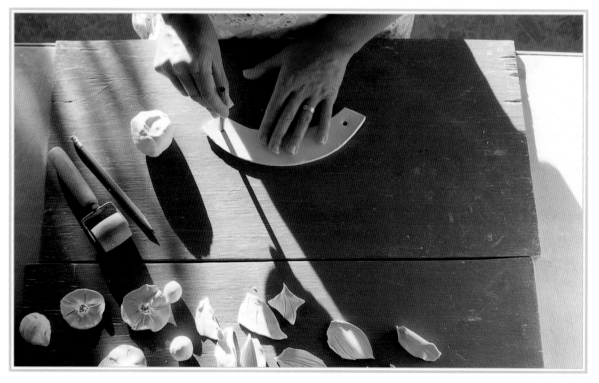

Poke a hole in each end of arch with the base of a needle tool.

To create flowers, roll out small balls of clay between palms, flatten, shape, and scribe with pencil tip. To form center of flower, roll a smaller ball of clay and place in center. Poke small ball with pencil point. To create leaves, roll out a thin slab of clay with a rolling pin and cut out leaf shapes with needle tool. Create texture with a pencil point. After creating enough flowers and leaves to cover arch, arrange and press firmly to secure pieces to arch.

Bake as directed on package. Paint with acrylic paints. Apply base coat, let dry. Add details.

Leaf Dish

Create a new leaf and relish it!

Materials  ✳ ≡ * 🍃 *

Clay, about 3 lbs.
Clay cutter
Clear glaze
Fresh leaf
Needle tool
Plastic bowl or plaster mold
Rolling pin (Once used for clay, retire
   from food use.)

Small bowl of water
Small roller
Sponge
Thin plastic
Underglaze in desired colors (We used
   honey, lavender, leaf green, peach, rose,
   and turquoise.)

* Not for food use.

Slice off about 3 lbs. of clay with a clay cutter. Roll out clay with a rolling pin to ¼" thick
slab, bigger than leaf you will be using (see photos, page 29). Place leaf on slab.

Pearl *The back of the leaf creates a deeper relief.*

Roll leaf with a rolling pin.

Roll leaf edge with a small roller to get a good, clear edge.

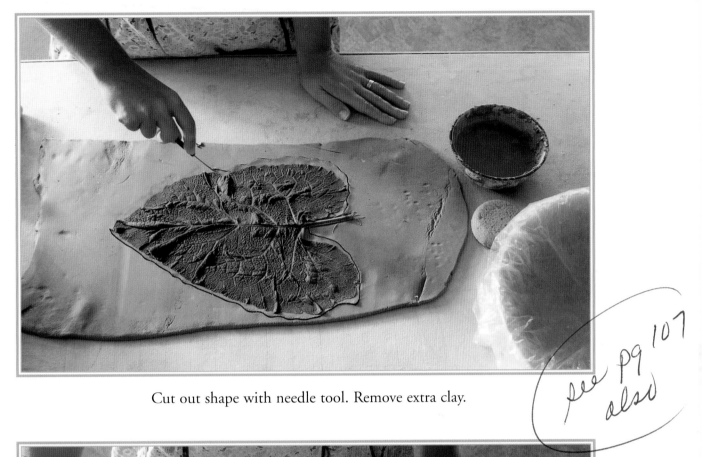

Cut out shape with needle tool. Remove extra clay.

see pg 107 also

Roll edge with a small roller.

Peel off leaf. Smooth edges with a damp sponge.

Place clay in shallow plastic bowl that has been lined with thin plastic (so it will not stick).
Press down gently. This is an example of a slump-mold technique.

Cover clay edge/lip with plastic to retard drying. Dry slowly to prevent cracking. Bisque fire to recommended temperature. Glaze and glaze fire (see Glazing Instructions, pages 39 and 51).

So easy a four-year-old can do it! We rolled out the slab and Mary Heather did the rest "all by herself."

"Look mom, I did it with my own hands!"

Instead of laying clay leaf inside a plastic bowl (slump-mold), Mary Heather laid hers *over* a plaster hump-mold. This method allows the texture on the outside of the dish, while the first method's texture is on the inside of the dish.

Mary Heather happily applied the underglaze to her leaf dish. We applied two coats of clear glaze* to seal the surface, making it safe for her to use with food.

Clear glaze is food safe after firing as directed, however, it does contain a small amount of lead silicate. We do not recommend any child be allowed to work with glazes containing lead.

Pinched Flower Finial

Use your pinched flower finial for a hose guide or decorative splash of color in garden or potted plant. If you make these to catch water, birds will visit for a welcome sip.

Materials ☀ ≡* 🍃*

Clay, about 1 lb.
Clay cutter
Dowel, ½" (We used a large wooden
   fork handle.)

Pencil, dull point
Small bowl of water
Sponge

* For indoor use only.

Slice off about 1 lb. of clay with a clay cutter (see photo, page 29). Roll out a thick tapered coil about 1½" in diameter at small end and about 3" in diameter at big end.

Press firmly with a thumb.

Make another deep impression right next to the first one, and so on all around the end.

Poke center multiple times with pencil point.

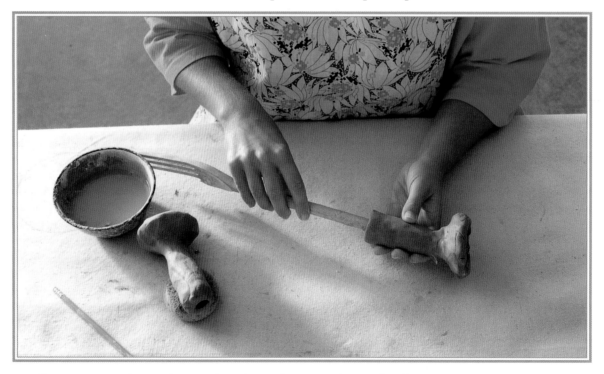

Hollow out stem by pushing a dowel into bottom about 5". This is to accommodate a stick when finished. Be careful not to go too far or it will go out the other end. Tidy up with a damp sponge. Dry slowly. Bisque fire to recommended temperature. Glaze and glaze fire (see Glazing Instructions, pages 39 and 51).

Cut Petal Flower Finial

A petal flower finial sets the mood and marks the spot for summer posies.

Materials ✳ ≡* 🍃*

Clay, about 1 lb.
Clay cutter
Dowel, ½" (We used a wooden fork handle.)
Needle tool

Pencil, medium point
Rolling pin (Once used for clay, retire
   from food use.)
Small bowl of water
Sponge

* For indoor use only.

Slice off about 1 lb. of clay with a clay cutter (see photo, page 29). Roll out a thick tapered coil about 1½" in diameter at small end and about 3" in diameter at big end.

Roll out clay with a rolling pin to ⅛" thick slab, about 3" x 9". Cut out petals with a needle tool.

Smooth edges with a damp sponge or finger.

Press one end of petal against end of coil and smooth with fingers.

Pearl *No scoring is needed because you have smoothed away seam.*

Overlap next petal slightly, press, and smooth. Continue this all around the end. Attach a bug if you like. Add details to bug with pencil point (see closeup, page 75). Hollow out handle with dowel. Dry slowly. Bisque fire to recommended temperature. Glaze and glaze fire (see Glazing Instructions, pages 39 and 51).

Shown above is a closeup of a ladybug. Begin with a small ball of clay. Add details with a pencil point.

Display your kiln-fired finials amid flowers in your own garden. Oven-bake and air-dry finials can be displayed in pots indoors.

Lattice Basket (Bowl)

The idea of weaving clay is ancient. Reminiscent of delicate Wedgewood porcelain baskets, these woven earthenware lattice baskets await daily use.

Pearl *This technique may be used to make a basket with a handle.*

Materials ☀ ≡* 🍃*

Clay, about 4 lbs.
Clay cutter
Fork (Once used for clay, retire from food use.)
Needle tool
Rolling pin (Once used for clay, retire from food use.)

Shallow plastic bowl for slump-mold
Small bowl of water
Sponge
Thin plastic
Wooden meat tenderizer (Once used for clay, retire from food use.)
Yardstick

* Not for food use.

Slice off about 4 lbs. of clay with a clay cutter (see photo, page 29). Roll out clay with a rolling pin to ¼" thick slab, about 18" x 20".

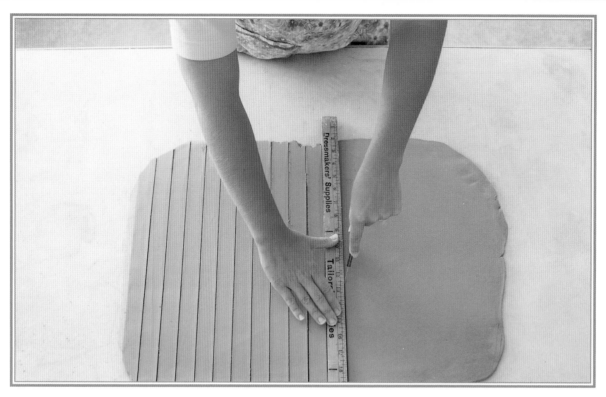

Cut strips the width of a yard stick with a needle tool.

Separate clay strips, soften and smooth edges with a damp sponge.

Arrange strips in rows ¾" apart. Lay another strip at right angle on top. Add strips, lifting every other one to weave.

When you get to the middle, gently fold back every other one. Lay a strip across. Fold strips back down on top, then fold back opposite ones. Repeat.

Press strips together by rolling gently with a rolling pin.

Line "mold" (shallow plastic bowl) with thin plastic.

Carefully lift woven clay into bowl.

Press down little by little on bottom and edges.

Cut clay around top edge of bowl with a needle tool.

Roll clay scraps into a long coil. Create texture by tapping with a meat tenderizer.

Score coil and top edge of basket with a fork.

Press coil onto top edge of basket and cut away extra clay. Smooth edge with damp sponge or finger. Dry slowly. Bisque fire to recommended temperature. Glaze and glaze fire (see Glazing Instructions, pages 39 and 51).

Stamped Buttons

Grandmother's fruitcake tin of buttons was the child-minder most remembered. Hours were spent sorting out the prettiest ones.

Materials ✳ ≡* 🍃*

Clay, about 8 oz. for 6 buttons
Circle cutter
Clay cutter
Pencil, medium point

Rolling pin (Once used for clay, retire
   from food use.)
Small bowl of water
Sponge
Stamp or button for texture

* Not as durable as kiln fire clay.

Slice off about 8 oz. of clay with a clay cutter. Roll out clay with a rolling pin to ¼" thick slab, large enough for the desired number of buttons (see photos, page 29). Stamp out circle with a circle cutter.

Press firmly with a stamp or button to make an impression.

Make holes with a pencil point. Remember, clay shrinks, so make certain holes are large enough. To clean up hole, also push pencil in from back.

Smooth edges with a damp sponge or finger. Spackle when dry. Bisque fire to recommended temperature. Glaze and glaze fire (see Glazing Instructions, pages 39 and 51). Hand wash gently or remove buttons before any laundering.

Beads can also be made using this technique. To make a hole in the bead, use a sharp pencil point or needle tool and spackle when dry.

Cut Buttons

The only fastener better than a shell button is a handmade clay *bouton*. Every tuffet needs a juicy button!

Materials ☀ ☰* 🍃*

Clay, about 8 oz. for 6 buttons
Clay cutter
Lace (or something for texture)
Needle tool
Pencil, medium point

Rolling pin (Once used for clay, retire from food use.)
Small bowl of water
Small roller
Sponge

* Not as durable as kiln fire clay.

Slice off about 8 oz. of clay with a clay cutter. Roll out clay with a rolling pin to ¼" thick slab large enough for the desired number of buttons (see photos, page 29). Press lace into clay with a small roller.

Cut out shape with a needle tool.

Smooth edges with damp sponge or finger.

Make holes with a pencil point. Remember, clay shrinks, so make certain holes are large enough. To clean up hole, also push pencil in from back. Spackle when dry. Bisque fire to recommended temperature. Glaze and glaze fire (see Glazing Instructions, pages 39 and 51). Hand wash gently or remove buttons before any laundering.

Beads can also be made using this technique. To make a hole in the bead, use a sharp pencil point or needle tool and spackle when dry.

Pressed Buttons

What's sweeter than handmade buttons on a toasty sweater, wool béret, or jumper.

Materials ✳ ≡ * 🍃*

Clay, about 8 oz. for 6 buttons
Clay cutter
Pencil, medium point

Small bowl of water
Sponge
Stamp or button for texture

* Not as durable as kiln fire clay.

Slice off about 8 oz. of clay with a clay cutter. Roll a small ball of stiff clay between palms.

Pinch flat.

If edges crack, smooth them with a damp sponge.

Press design with stamp, button, or whatever.

Make holes with a pencil point. Remember, clay shrinks, so make certain holes are large enough. To clean up hole, also push pencil in from back. Spackle when dry. Bisque fire to recommended temperature. Glaze and glaze fire (see Glazing Instructions, pages 39 and 51). Hand wash gently or remove buttons before any laundering.

Bottle Chiller

Be the cordial host, ready with a drink cooling in clay at your autumn table.

Materials ✳

Clay, about 6½ lbs.
Clay cutter
Empty oatmeal box or a round cardboard
  container
Fork (Once used for clay, retire from
  food use.)
Needle tool

Paper (We used telephone book paper.)
Pencil, dull point
Rolling pin (Once used for clay, retire
  from food use.)
Small bowl of water
Sponge
Yardstick

This cylinder pot may be made shorter to be used as a kitchen utensil holder.
Our finished bottle chiller measures 9¼" tall with a 5¼" diameter.

Pearl *We like to use telephone book paper because it's nice and flat, the ink does not come off
on your hands, and its crisp surface repels water.*

Slice off about 6½ lbs. of clay with a clay cutter. Roll out clay with a rolling pin to ⅓" thick
slab, about 16" x 20" (see photos, page 29). On one edge of slab, cut a circle with a needle
tool slightly larger than the bottom of the box. Score edge of circle with a fork.

Trim slab with a needle tool to the height of the box. Wrap paper around box.

Roll slab around the box.

Score slab with a fork where edges will meet.

Apply slip. Roll so scored areas meet.

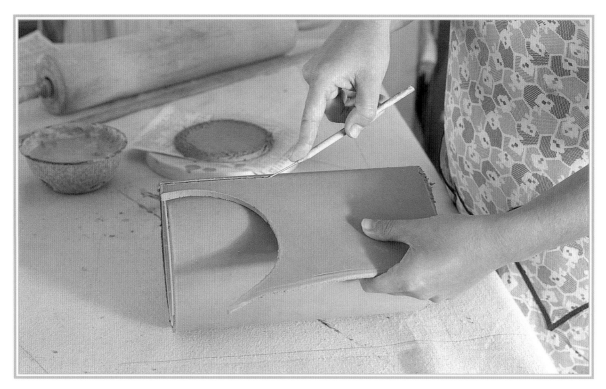

Cut off extra clay with a needle tool.

Score bottom of cylinder with a fork. Apply slip to scored edges of cylinder and circle.

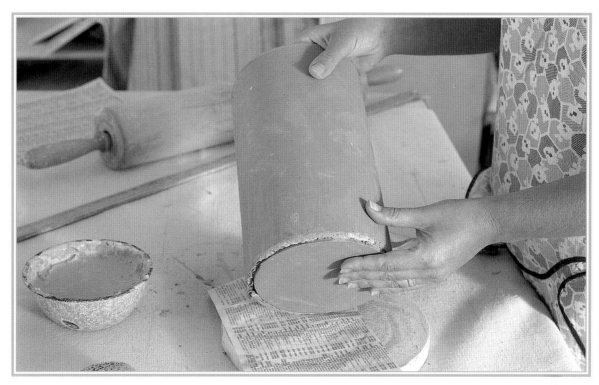

Place cylinder on scored circle.

Press and clean seams with a damp sponge.

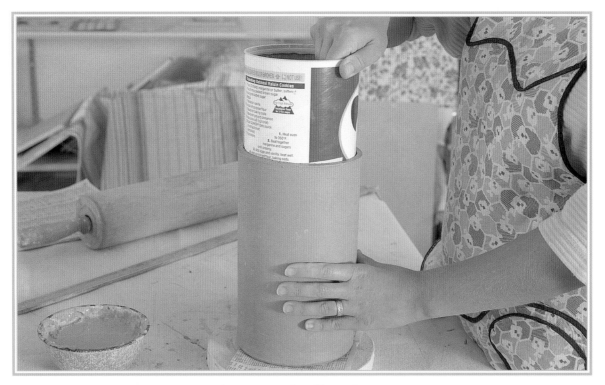

Flip over and pull out box.

Pull out paper. To ensure a watertight seal see instructions, page 36.

To create decorative edge, roll out two clay coils about 18" long.

Twist coils together.

Score the length on one side of the twisted coils and the top of the cylinder with a fork.

Place twisted coil element on pot. Press in place. Cut off extra with a needle tool.

Allow bottle chiller to stiffen a bit. Draw a design on outside of bottle chiller with a pencil point. When leather hard, clean up the decorative top with a pencil point and a damp sponge. Carving can also be done at this time with the pencil point. Dry slowly to prevent cracking. Bisque fire to recommended temperature. Glaze and glaze fire (see Glazing Instructions, pages 39 and 51).

The handbuilding techniques we've described will allow you to create many projects of your own design. Here are some projects we would like to share with you.

Knobs

Garnets, turquoise, coral, wood, shell, and seed bead necklaces hang in total organization. Together, they await the next occasion.

Materials ☀ ≡ * 🍃 *

Clay, about 1 oz.
Fork (Retire from food use.)
Needle tool
Pencil, medium point

Shown here as jewelry organizers, these knobs may also be used for cabinet and drawer pulls.

* Not as durable as kiln-fire clay.

1. Pinch a small amount of clay into desired knob shape. Flatten base.

2. Create flowers and leaves (see flower construction, page 46).

3. Score, slip, and attach flowers and leaves to top of knob.

4. Make 2-3 screw holes through base with a pencil. Dry slowly to prevent cracking. Bisque fire to recommended temperature. Glaze and glaze fire (see Glazing Instructions, pages 39 and 51).

Small Leaf Pot

Though the daffodils will turn to dust, the memory of the small geranium leaves that inspired this pot will last and last.

Materials ✳ ≡* 🍃*

Clay, about 1 lb.
Clay cutter
Fork (Retire from food use.)
Needle tool
Rolling pin (Retire from food use.)
Small bowl of water
Sponge
Small leaves (We used geranium *(fresh from plant)* leaves.)
Small roller

* Not for food use.

1. Slice off about 1 lb. of clay with a clay cutter. Roll out clay with a rolling pin to ¼" thick slab, large enough for five or six leaves.

2. Place leaves on the slab. Roll leaves with a rolling pin.

3. Cut around leaves with a needle tool. To get a good clear edge, roll edges of leaves with small roller. Remove leaves.

4. Make base by flattening small ball of clay to 2½" diameter circle.

5. Score base and leaves only where overlapping. Apply slip. Attach the leaves to base, overlapping enough to create a pot shape.

6. Dry slowly to prevent cracking. Bisque fire to recommended temperature. Glaze and glaze fire (see Glazing Instructions, pages 39 and 51).

Chicken Planter

After all, eggs are just perfect! They are a perfect container and prized gift in many cultures. Likewise, the chicken on her nest, brooding and clucking, is the picture of nurturing diligence.

Materials ✳

Clay, about 7 lbs.
Clay cutter
Fork (Once used for clay, retire from food use.)

Needle tool
Oval pattern
Paper
Pencil, sharp point

Rolling pin (Once used for clay, retire from food use.)
Small bowl of water/sponge
Thin plastic
Tongue depressor

1. Slice off about 7 lbs. of clay with a clay cutter. Roll out clay with a rolling pin to ½" thick slab, about 10" x 12" (large enough for base). Cut the slab into an oval shape with pattern and needle tool.

2. Roll out coils ½" thick. Score oval base and a coil. Apply slip. Attach coil to oval base. Build up wall to about 7" (see coiling, page 44). Cover lip with plastic to keep moist, allowing the rest to firm up.

Pearl *Too tall and the wall will sag. Wait until the clay stiffens before adding more coils.*

3. Smooth coils with a tongue depressor inside and out. Continue to add coils.

Pearl *When smoothing coils, support wall with your other hand so when you are pushing against the coils you maintain the shape. Wall should go out and in (see diagram at right).*

4. Create a tail with slightly smaller coils. Support coils as they go across by rolling up some paper, bend paper over and use this to hold up coil. This will be removed as soon as clay is dry enough to support itself (depending on the amount of humidity, usually about one day).

5. When clay is leather hard, create texture with the tongue depressor by dabbing at the surface. For smaller marks like the hackle feathers around the neck, dab in marks with the eraser end of the pencil. To form the comb on top of head, pinch with fingers. Poke holes for eyes with pencil point. Add a tiny ball of clay into eye hole if you like.

6. If side pockets are desired, slice a shape through side of chicken with a needle tool (see diagram at right). Gently pinch out to thin clay with fingers and form a pocket.

Cut this shape to form a pocket

Push in

Pull out

7. Cover loosely with thin plastic. Dry slowly to prevent cracking. Bisque fire to recommended temperature. Glaze and glaze fire (see Glazing Instructions, pages 39 and 51).

Wee Clay Hats

Skimmers these hats could be called. Worn in the garden or to a summer soirée, they are essential to every woman's ensemble. Fine ribbons sail on a breeze amidst anemones, daisies, and bluebells.

Materials ✳ ≡ 🍃
Clay, about 1 oz.
Pencil
Small bowl of water

1. Work clay with palms in a rolling, flattening motion to create a smooth shape.

2. Pinch all around edge to create brim, leaving middle up. Roll edge of hat brim with the ferrule of a pencil eraser. These ridges create the straw-like texture.

3. Put hat upside down on flat surface. Push in center of hat with eraser end of pencil. Wiggle around in a circular motion to enlarge opening. Tidy up texture with eraser ferrule.

4. Create a hat band by flattening a small coil (make certain clay is moist enough to bend). If it starts to crack, apply a small amount of water with fingertip.

5. Decorate as you like with flowers, fruit, or whatever (see flower construction, page 46). Dry slowly to prevent cracking. Bisque fire to recommended temperature. Glaze and glaze fire (see Glazing Instructions, pages 39 and 51).

Tile

Tile has presence, permanence, and durability. Tile is reminiscent of kitchens with wood burning stoves and gas light. We are so lucky to mix that old flavor with the beauty of stainless ranges and refrigerators, food processors, bread makers, and blenders. Old with new, tile evokes thoughts of both.

There are entire books available on this subject. For a basic method try this, it works for us!

Materials ✳

Clay, about 5½ lbs. for six 4½" square tiles	Clay cutter	Pencil, dull point
	Cloth covered board	Plaster wall board
Carpenter's square	Lace (or something for texture)	Rolling pin (Retire from food use.)
	Needle tool	Small bowl of water/sponge

Pearl *When rolling out a slab for tile, it's vital not to bend it, or the clay will warp when bisque fired. To avoid warping, roll the slab on a cloth covered board. Place another board on top and flip the whole thing over to lift it off. Drying tile between pieces of plaster wallboard helps tile to dry flat.*

1. Slice off with a clay cutter enough clay for the number of tiles you wish to make. Roll out clay with a rolling pin to ¼" thick slab. Standard tiles are 4¼" or 6¼" square. However, you may make tiles any size. To make a 4¼" square tile, cut tile to 4½" square (for 6¼" square tile, cut tile to 6½"). Clay shrinks! Lay carpenter's square on slab, cut by following edge of carpenter's square with a needle tool to achieve a true right angle.

2. Cut out as many tiles as you wish. Remove scraps from around tiles so edges can dry.

3. To decorate tiles there are many options:
    ❦ make a lace impression before cutting (see instructions, page 31)
    ❦ draw original designs when tile is leather hard (see photo, page 105)
    ❦ create designs with glaze techniques on bisqued tile

4. Dry slowly to prevent cracking. Spackle. Bisque fire to recommended temperature. Glaze and glaze fire (see Glazing Instructions, pages 39 and 51.)

1. Slice off about 1½ lbs. of clay with a clay cutter. Roll out clay with a rolling pin to ¼" thick slab to the desired dimensions. Cut desired shape and size from slab with a needle tool. Press lace into clay with a small roller.

2. For a square mirror/frame, use a carpenter's square as a guide to create a recess on back of mirror/frame with a loop tool by running the loop tool against the carpenter's square. This recess accommodates a mirror or picture. Because it is more difficult to cut a recess for a circular mirror, surface mount the mirror with clear caulk after the frame is glaze fired.

3. Dry slowly to prevent cracking. Spackle. Bisque fire to recommended temperature. Glaze and glaze fire (see Glazing Instructions, pages 39 and 51).

4. Attach mirror to back of frame with clear caulk. When caulk is dry, finish by gluing felt over the back of mirror. Be certain to cut felt with a scissors to cover mirror edges about ½".

Pearl *See Tile, page 112, for information on warp prevention.*

Mirrors & Frames

In the East, mirrors are used to expand space and to give infinite possibilities for observation. In the West, it's always handy to have a mirror nearby to reapply one's lipstick before going downstairs to meet guests.

Materials ❋ ≡ ❧
Clay, about 1½ lbs. for a 4" x 6" frame or about 3 lbs. for a 10" diameter frame.
Carpenter's square
Clay cutter
Clear caulk
Craft glue
Felt
Lace (or something for texture)

Slump or Hump Molded Plates & Bowls

Eating from a favorite bowl, a handmade vessel, is a pleasure.

Materials ✳ ≡* ◑*

Clay, about 3 lbs. for an 8" bowl
Clay cutter
Lace (or something for texture)
Lid or cardboard

Needle tool
Rolling pin (Retire from food use.)
Scissors
Slump mold
Thin plastic

Slump/hump molded plates are made by laying slab rolled clay over or inside of plaster molds or anything that is shallow (plate, bowl, or whatever). We have used plates and bowls found at yard sales.

* Not for food use.

1. Slice off about 3 lbs. of clay with a clay cutter. Roll out clay with a rolling pin to $\frac{1}{4}$" thick slab, about 12" square slab for an 8" plate. If texture is desired, lay lace on slab and roll with rolling pin

2. Cut a pattern from cardboard with scissors, using a plate, bowl, or lid as a sizing guide. Place pattern on clay. Cut clay around the pattern with a needle tool.

3. Place thin plastic inside or over mold. Lay clay in or over mold. Tamp down gently to keep texture sharp. Dry slowly to prevent cracking. Spackle. Bisque fire to recommended temperature. Glaze and glaze fire (see Glazing Instructions, pages 39 and 51).

Little Chickens

Decorating with farm fowl, big and little, nestless or brooding, creates a chintzed elegance bridging farm and town.

Materials ✳ ≡ 🍃
Clay, about 2-3 oz.
Pencil
Needle tool
Small bowl of water
Sponge

Pearl *These instructions can be used for clay cats, birds, or whatever you can imagine!*

1. Pinch a small amount of clay into chicken shape.

2. Hollow out from underneath by pushing eraser end of pencil in center and wiggling around a bit.

3. Close up hole by smoothing a tiny slab of clay over it.

4. Pierce underside with needle tool to release air during firing or piece will explode.

5. Dry slowly to prevent cracking. Spackle. Bisque fire to recommended temperature. Glaze and glaze fire (see Glazing Instructions, pages 39 and 51).

Shoes

We're too sensible and busy these days to wear fussy ankle benders, but pumps harking to Louis the 14th could work – low to the ground, but with plenty of frills and beads.

Materials ☀ ≡ 🍃
Clay, about 1 oz.
Lace (or something for texture)
Loop tool
Needle tool
Pencil, medium point
Small bowl of water/sponge

1. Shoes are made with a combination of pinching and shaping. Pinch out the basic shape.

2. Hollow clay out of the body with a loop tool. Smooth and continue to shape with fingers.

3. Shape outside by cutting clay away with a needle tool. Add embellishments as desired and/or press with texture while clay is still moist. Add details with a pencil point when leather dry.

4. Dry slowly. Spackle. Bisque fire to recommended temperature. Glaze and glaze fire (see Glazing Instructions, pages 39 and 51).

Curtain Tiebacks

A fancy, old idea made anew.

Materials ✳ ≡ 🍃
Clay, about 1 lb. for two 3" tiebacks
Clay cutter
Dowel, one 3½" long 1" diameter for each
   tieback
Drill (optional)
Epoxy glue
Lace (or something for texture)
Needle tool
Pliers
Rolling pin (Retire from food use.)
Screw threaded at both ends, one for each
   tieback
Small bowl of water/sponge
Small roller

1. Slice off about 1 lb. of clay with a clay cutter. Roll out clay with a rolling pin to ¼" thick slab, about 8" square.

2. Press lace into clay with a small roller, if texture is desired. Cut desired shape with a needle tool.

3. Dry slowly to prevent cracking. Bisque fire. Glaze and glaze fire (see Glazing Instructions, pages 39 and 51).

4. After glaze firing, attach dowel to back with epoxy glue.

5. When glue is set, screw double-threaded dowel screw half way in with pliers. Take care not to alter threads with pliers.

Pearl *It is easier to insert screw into dowel if you first drill a hole slightly smaller then the screw you are using.*

Nest & Eggs

Create a quaint clutch of cackleberries – sheer whimsy!

Materials ✳ ≡ 🍃
Clay, about 1 oz.
Pencil, sharp point

1. Roll a small amount of clay into a ball with palms.

2. Press in center of ball with eraser end of pencil. Create texture on outside of nest with a pencil point.

3. Roll teenie tiny balls for eggs.

4. Dry. Bisque fire to recommended temperature. Glaze and glaze fire (see Glazing Instructions, pages 39 and 51).

Scrap Pot

Cast off, but not forgotten. These odds and ends, playfully pinched together, make a faultless container for whatnots.

Materials ✳ ≡* 🍃*

Clay, about 10 oz. of scraps
Container for molding

Lace (or something for texture)
Small bowl of water/sponge
Thin plastic

Your scrap pot could turn out lovely or not, it's only mud and time...but ooh what fun!

Not for food use.

1. Take any leftover clay slab scraps, and if texture is desired press lace into clay with a small roller.

2. Playfully press into a container lined with thin plastic. Add embellishments if desired.

3. Dry slowly to prevent cracking. Spackle. Bisque fire to recommended temperature. Glaze and glaze fire (see Glazing Instructions, pages 39 and 51).

Gallery of Possibilities

It is impossible to include all of the things you can make with the techniques in this book. The following photos are examples of advanced projects, and some of our favorite things. With experience all of the projects in the gallery could be made using these techniques. We encourage you to experiment and use your imagination. Handbuilding with clay has limitless possibilities.